DEVONSHIRE
RECIPES

compiled by
Amanda Persey

with illustrations
by A. R. Quinton

SALMON

Index

Cover pictures *front:* East Budleigh
back: Rose Cottage, Clovelly
Title page: Cottages at Cockington

Printed and Published by J. Salmon Ltd., Sevenoaks, England © Copyright

Devon Apple Cake

8 oz. self-raising flour (try using half white and half wholemeal flour)
1 teaspoon ground cinnamon   1 teaspoon mixed spice
4 oz. soft brown or caster sugar   4 oz. butter
2 large cooking apples, peeled, cored and diced
1 medium egg

Set oven to 375°F or Mark 5. Grease and line an 8 inch cake tin. Mix together all the dry ingredients in a large bowl. Rub in the butter until the mixture resembles fine breadcrumbs. Stir in the apples and lastly the egg. Mix well. Pour the mixture into the tin. Bake for 30-40 minutes until risen, firm and golden in colour. This cake is delicious served warm as a pudding with lashings of clotted cream.

Dartmouth Pie

1½ lb. of leg of pork, cut into thin slices
3 medium onions, peeled and sliced
3 large cooking apples, peeled, cored and sliced
2 tablespoons brown sugar mixed with a pinch of ground nutmeg
and a pinch of ground cinnamon
½ pint dry cider
8 oz. shortcrust pastry

Set oven to 400°F or Mark 6. Place a layer of thinly sliced pork in a deep oven-proof dish. Cover this with a layer of apples and then half of the sugar-and-spice mixture. On top of the sugar place a layer of onions. Repeat these three layers and then pour the cider over all. Roll out the pastry on a floured surface and use to cover the dish, making two holes for the steam to escape; or use a pie funnel. Bake for 20 minutes. Reduce the oven temperature to 300°F or Mark 2. Cover the pastry with foil to prevent burning and continue the cooking for a further 60 minutes. Serve hot with warm clotted cream.

Teddy Soup

2 medium sized potatoes, peeled and chopped
1 medium sized leek, peeled, sliced and washed
1 oz. butter   1 pint good chicken stock
½ pint full cream milk
1 teaspoon mixed herbs
Salt and pepper

Teddy is a Devon term for potatoes. Melt the butter in a large saucepan, put in the prepared vegetables, cover and sweat for 10 minutes (they should not brown at all). Add the stock, cream and herbs and bring to the boil. Reduce the heat and simmer gently for about 30 minutes until the potatoes are very soft. Liquidise or rub through a sieve and, if desired, thin with more milk. Season to taste and reheat to the required temperature.

Devonshire Splits

½ oz. fresh yeast	1 lb. strong white flour
1 teaspoon caster sugar	1 oz. caster sugar
½ pint milk – warmed to blood heat	1 teaspoon salt
2 oz. butter	

Mix together the yeast, the 1 teaspoon of sugar and the warm milk and leave in a warm place for 20-30 minutes until frothy. Rub the butter into the flour and stir in the 1 oz. of sugar and the salt. Add the yeast liquid to the flour and mix to a soft dough. Knead on a floured surface until smooth and elastic. Leave covered in a warm place for about 1 hour until doubled in size. Knock back, knead again and divide into 16 pieces. Mould into neat bun shapes and place on floured baking sheets. Leave once again in a warm place until well risen. Bake in a pre-heated oven at 425°F or Mark 7 for approximately 15 minutes until pale golden in colour. Cool on a wire rack. These sweet dough buns are often served with a traditional clotted cream tea. They are split and filled with the cream and home-made jam.

Chocolate Fudge Pudding

PUDDING
4 oz. butter   **4 oz. caster sugar**   **2 medium eggs**   **3 oz. self-raising flour**
2 tablespoons cocoa powder   **½ teaspoon vanilla essence**   **1-2 tablespoons milk**

SAUCE
4 oz. soft brown sugar   **2 tablespoons cocoa powder**
½ pint boiling water

Set oven to 375°F or Mark 5. Place all the pudding ingredients into a bowl and beat well to a soft consistency or use a food processor. Put into a 2½ pint baking dish. Make the sauce by combining the sugar and cocoa in a bowl and adding the hot water. Mix well. Pour this sauce over the pudding mixture. Bake for 40 minutes. Turn out the pudding and you will find a thick chocolate sauce has formed, coating a light sponge pudding. It is delicious served with thick cream.

UINTON

Hedgerow Jelly

1 lb. blackberries   1 lb. elderberries   1 lb. crab apples
8 oz. sloes   Water   Granulated sugar

Prepare the fruit by washing it all and cutting up the crab apples roughly. An easy way to remove the elderberries from the stem is to pull through the prongs of a fork. Place the fruit into a thick-based pan and just cover with water. Simmer slowly until all the fruit is very mushy. Strain through a jelly bag – it is best to leave this overnight. Do not squeeze the bag or the resulting jelly will be cloudy. Measure the juice and place in a clean, thick-based pan. Add 1 lb. granulated sugar for each pint of juice extract. Stir over a gentle heat until the sugar has dissolved and then boil rapidly until setting point is reached (220°F). Pour into clean, warm jam jars and cover in the usual way.

Devon Clotted Cream Biscuits

8 oz. thick farmhouse clotted cream   **1 large egg**
1 lb. flour   **8 oz. caster sugar**
1-2 tablespoons milk

Set oven to 400°F or Mark 6. Place the clotted cream in a large mixing bowl and sieve in the flour. Add the egg, stirring with a round-ended knife until the mixture resembles fine breadcrumbs. Add 3 oz. of the sugar and enough milk to make a pastry consistency. Roll thinly on a lightly floured surface and cut into rounds. Sprinkle with the remaining caster sugar. Place on a floured baking sheet and bake for approximately 15 minutes until pale golden in colour. Cool slightly before transferring to a wire rack. These are delicious crisp, creamy biscuits.

Devonshire Fish Casserole

1½ pints dry cider   1 oz. butter   1 large onion, peeled and diced
4 oz. button mushrooms   1½ lb. monk fish, skinned and cut into cubes
1 oz. flour   1 tablespoon fresh parsley, finely chopped
1 teaspoon marjoram, finely chopped   Salt and pepper
2 tablespoons single cream

Set oven to 325°F or Mark 3. Boil the cider rapidly in a saucepan to reduce it to 1 pint. In a separate pan melt the butter, add the onion and cook for 3 minutes. Add the mushrooms and fish and cook for 1 minute, then add the flour and stir well. Pour the cider over, stir well and add the herbs; season to taste. Transfer to a casserole dish and bake for 30 minutes (or continue to cook on top of the cooker for 30 minutes). Stir in the cream just before serving. Serve with fresh vegetables and crusty bread.

Parsnip Cakes

4 medium parsnips, cooked and mashed **1 medium egg, beaten**
4 tablespoons self-raising flour **Freshly ground black pepper**
2 oz. butter for frying

Well mix together all the ingredients and on a floured surface and shape into even-sized cakes. Heat the butter and fry the cakes on both sides until brown and crisp. Drain on kitchen paper and serve hot. These cakes can be made in advance, stored in the refrigerator and cooked as required. They also freeze well and provide an interesting and tasty accompaniment to many dishes. Try them with Devon Roast Lamb or Upcott Pork.

Harvest Pudding

6-8 slices of buttered bread, medium-sliced
1 lb. cooking apples, peeled, cored and sliced
2 oz. shredded suet   3 oz. soft brown sugar
2 oz. raisins   Grated rind of one lemon
2 medium eggs   ½ pint milk

Line a pie dish with some of the buttered bread. Mix together the apples, suet, sugar, raisins and lemon rind. Fill the pie dish with the mixture and cover with more buttered bread (buttered side uppermost). Beat together the eggs and milk and pour over the top of the bread. Cover and leave to stand in a cool place for approximately 2 hours. Bake in a pre-heated oven at 350°F or Mark 4 for approximately 1 hour. Serve warm with clotted cream.

Exeter Stew *with Savoury Doughballs*

STEW

2 lb. stewing beef	½ swede, peeled and diced
2 medium onions, peeled and diced	2 pints beef stock
2 medium carrots, peeled and sliced	2 oz. flour
1 small turnip, peeled and diced	2 oz. lard or oil/butter mix for frying

DOUGHBOYS

6 oz. flour   4 oz. suet   ½ teaspoon baking powder
Freshly chopped herbs (thyme and parsley)
Salt and pepper   Cold water to mix

Doughboy is the Devon name for dumpling. This tasty stew provides a substantial meal for a winter's day. Prepare the meat by removing any fat and cutting into cubes. Melt the fat and fry the meat until brown. Add the vegetables and fry for a further few minutes. Stir in the flour and then add the stock, season and simmer in a covered pan for 1-1½ hours. Meanwhile prepare the doughboys by mixing together the flour, suet, baking powder and seasoning. Stir in the herbs and add sufficient water to make a soft dough. Shape into 8-10 small balls and add to the stew; they will swell whilst cooking. Continue cooking for a further 25 minutes or until the meat is tender.

Mol's Coffee House, Exeter

Sticky Toffee Pudding

PUDDING

8oz 2 oz. butter 4 x 1 medium egg

1½lb 6 oz. caster sugar 11½lb 6 oz. stoned dates, roughly chopped

2lb 8 oz. flour 2pt ½ pint boiling water

4 1 teaspoon baking powder 4 1 teaspoon bicarbonate of soda

4 1 teaspoon vanilla essence

TOFFEE SAUCE

8oz — 2 oz. butter 3 oz. soft brown sugar -12oz.

8 — 2 tablespoons double or single cream

Set oven to 350°F or Mark 4. Pour the boiling water over the dates and bicarbonate of soda and leave to stand. Cream the butter and sugar together in a bowl until pale in colour. Gradually stir in the egg, flour and baking powder. Stir in the dates with the liquid and lastly the vanilla essence. Bake for approximately 40 minutes until risen and firm to the touch. Make the sauce by boiling the ingredients together for 2 minutes and pour over the warm pudding.

Devonshire Cider Cake

4 oz. caster sugar	8 oz. self-raising flour
4 oz. butter	1 teaspoon cinnamon
2 medium eggs	½ pint cider

Set oven to 350°F or Mark 4. Grease and line an 8 inch round cake tin. Cream the sugar and butter together in a bowl until pale in colour. Stir in the eggs, cinnamon and half of the flour. Gradually add the cider to this mixture and lastly add the remaining flour and mix thoroughly. Pour into the tin and bake for approximately 45 minutes until firm to the touch and golden in colour.

Salcombe Crab Soup

1 oz. butter   2 sticks celery, trimmed and chopped
1 medium onion, peeled and diced
1 clove garlic, peeled and crushed
¼ pint dry white wine   1 pint good fish stock
1 bay leaf   1 teaspoon anchovy essence
Salt and freshly ground black pepper
1 lb. brown and white crab meat mixed, i.e. the cooked "meat" from two medium sized crabs
¼ pint single cream   1 tablespoon brandy or 2 tablespoons sherry

If fresh crab is not available, frozen crab meat can be used instead; thaw before use

Melt the butter in a large saucepan and gently cook the onion, garlic and celery until the onion is soft and transparent. Add the wine, the stock and the bay leaf, anchovy essence, salt and pepper. Boil rapidly for 5 minutes. Add the crab meat and simmer for a further 10 minutes. Remove the bay leaf and liquidise or whisk the mixture. Return to the pan and add the cream and the brandy or sherry. Warm through, but do not boil, and serve.

Clotted Cream Fudge

2 lb. soft brown sugar   **6 oz. clotted cream**
½ pint full cream milk   **Vanilla essence**

Grease a 12 inch x 4 inch (or equivalent size) baking tin. Put the sugar and milk in a thick-based pan and leave to stand for about 1 hour. Add the clotted cream and bring to the boil, stirring only enough to prevent burning. Boil rapidly for 10-15 minutes until the temperature reaches 240°F. Remove from the heat and leave to stand for 2 minutes. Then add a few drops of vanilla essence and beat to the consistency of thick cream. Pour into the tin and leave to cool. Mark into squares with a knife before completely cold.

Apple In and Out

8 oz. self-raising flour   4 oz. shredded suet
2 oz. caster sugar   Pinch of salt
2 large cooking apples, peeled, cored and cut into chunky pieces
Cold water to mix

Set oven to 350°F or Mark 4. Mix the dry ingredients together in a bowl and stir in the prepared apples. Add enough cold water to form a soft but not sticky dough. Put into a large, greased pie dish and bake for approximately 45 minutes until golden brown in colour.

Devon Herb Flan

8 oz. shortcrust pastry
4 oz. Curworthy cheese (or Cheddar), grated
2 rashers bacon, cut into small pieces
1 medium onion, peeled and diced
½ green pepper, deseeded and cut into small pieces
¼ pint milk   2 medium eggs   Salt and pepper
Fresh herbs to taste, washed and finely chopped;
(marjoram, thyme and parsley would all be suitable)

Set oven to 375°F or Mark 5. Grease an 8 inch flan dish. Roll out the pastry on a floured surface and use to line the dish. Bake blind for 10 minutes. Prepare the filling by gently frying together the bacon and onion. Mix together the milk, eggs, salt, pepper and herbs in a bowl. Spread the bacon and onion mixture together with the green pepper pieces over the base of the flan. Add three-quarters of the cheese to the milk/egg mixture and pour this over the filling. Top with the remaining cheese and bake in the oven for 30-40 minutes until well risen and golden in colour.

Deep Fried Cheeses with Gooseberry Sauce

A selection of cheeses cut into approximately 1 oz. portions:
most types of cheese are suitable (allow 3 oz. in total per person)
2 tablespoons seasoned flour   1 egg, beaten
4 oz. dried breadcrumbs
Oil for deep frying

GOOSEBERRY SAUCE
8 oz. gooseberries   1 oz. butter   2-4 tablespoons sugar according to taste

Prepare the gooseberry sauce by stewing the fruit in very little water until very soft. Sieve or purée in a blender. Stir in the butter and add sugar to taste. Set aside to cool.

Heat the oil to 375°F. Toss the pieces of cheese in the seasoned flour, then dip them in the egg and lastly coat with the breadcrumbs. Deep fry the cheeses (most types of cheese are suitable) until they are crisp on the outside, but still maintain their original shape. Drain on absorbent paper and keep hot while frying the remaining batches. Serve the cheeses hot with the cold gooseberry sauce as a starter. Redcurrant jelly can be used as an alternative to the gooseberry sauce.

Apple Scones

8 oz. wholemeal self-raising flour   1 teaspoon ground cinnamon
1 teaspoon baking powder   4 oz. butter
2 oz. soft brown sugar
2 medium sized cooking apples, peeled, cored and finely diced
1 medium egg

Set oven to 375°F or Mark 5. Mix the flour, cinnamon and baking powder together in a large bowl. Rub in the butter, stir in the sugar and apple and lastly stir in the egg. Mould into 10 or 12 heaps (as you would for rock buns) and place on a floured baking sheet. Bake for 20-25 minutes. Allow to cool slightly before transferring to a wire rack. Serve with butter.

Brixham Fish Soup

2 tablespoons olive oil   2 onions, peeled and sliced
2 cloves garlic, crushed   2 medium leeks, trimmed and sliced
2 medium carrots, peeled and sliced thinly   1 large can chopped tomatoes
1½ pints good fish stock   ½ pint dry white wine
2 bay leaves   Salt and pepper
2 lb. mixed fish fillets (monk fish, gurnard, cod, plaice, etc)
4 tablespoons double cream   1 tablespoon chopped parsley

Heat the oil in a large saucepan, add the onions and fry until softened. Add the garlic, leeks and carrots and cook for 2-3 minutes. Add the tomatoes, stock, wine and bay leaves. Season and simmer for 15 minutes. Prepare the fish by cutting into bite-size pieces. Add the firm fish first (for example monk fish) and cook for 3 minutes, then add the more delicate fish (for example plaice) and cook for a further 2 or 3 minutes. Do not overcook the fish. Pour the soup into a warmed dish, stir in the cream and sprinkle with parsley.

Fish soup or stew, which it almost resembles, can be made using fish according to the season and the catch. There are many variations.

Cider Toddy

½ pint dry cider   **A strip of lemon rind**
A piece of fresh root ginger   **1 tablespoon clear honey**

Put the cider, ginger and lemon rind into a pan and heat until hot, but not boiling. Stir in the honey and strain into a warmed glass. This makes a warming drink to enjoy on a cold winter's evening – very reviving.

Devonshire Junket

1 pint rich creamy milk **1-2 teaspoons brandy**
1-2 level tablespoons caster sugar **1 teaspoon liquid rennet**
Grated nutmeg

Warm the milk to blood heat and add the brandy and sugar. Pour into a serving dish and stir in the rennet. When set, spread thick Devonshire cream over the top and sprinkle with a little nutmeg. Be careful not to overheat the milk when making the junket nor to chill it too rapidly or it may not set.

Thatched Chicken Pie

¾-1 lb. cooked chicken	¼ pint dry cider
1 oz. flour	1 small onion, finely diced
1 oz. butter	Salt and pepper
½ pint milk	4 oz. Cheddar type cheese, grated

8 oz. shortcrust pastry

Set oven to 400°F or Mark 6. Melt the butter in a pan and add the flour. Cook for 2-3 minutes, stirring all the time. Remove from the heat and stir in the milk and cider, a little at a time. Return to the heat and continue stirring until the sauce thickens. Add the onion and cook for 5 minutes. Next add the cheese and lastly the chicken and seasoning. Place the mixture into a pie dish. Roll out the pastry on a floured surface and use to cover the dish. Cook for approximately 30 minutes, until the pastry is golden in colour.

Trout Baked in Paper Parcels
Served with Lemon Butter

4 fresh pink rainbow trout   Salt and freshly ground black pepper
Sprigs of fresh thyme and/or marjoram
4 large "heart-shaped" pieces of greaseproof paper

LEMON BUTTER
4 oz. butter   Rind and juice of half a lemon

To make the lemon butter, soften the butter and beat in the lemon rind and juice with a wooden spoon. Roll into a long sausage and wrap in greaseproof paper. Store in the refrigerator.

Gut and wash the trout carefully. Season well with salt and pepper and place some fresh herbs in the centre of each fish. Lay each fish on one half of a greaseproof paper "heart". Fold the paper over tightly and seal the edges by twisting the paper together, thus making a parcel. Place on a baking sheet and cook in a pre-heated oven at 425°F or Mark 7 for 15 minutes. As the paper is carefully removed the skin will peel away exposing the moist, pink flesh. Serve with lemon butter cut into thin slices.

Field Mushroom Soup

1 lb. fresh field mushrooms, washed and sliced roughly
2 medium onions, peeled and roughly chopped
1 pint white stock (chicken or vegetable)
2 oz. butter   2 oz. flour
1½ pints full cream milk   Salt and pepper

Cook the mushrooms and onions in the stock for about 30 minutes until tender. Rub this mixture through a sieve or purée in a food processor. Melt the butter in a separate pan, add the flour and cook gently for 2-3 minutes. Remove the pan from the heat and gradually stir in all the milk. Bring to the boil and stir until it thickens. Add the purée and return to the heat. Simmer for 30 minutes, season well and serve.

West Country Tart

6 oz. shortcrust pastry

FILLING
8 oz. golden syrup, slightly warmed   1 oz. soft brown sugar
3 oz. walnuts, finely chopped   2 medium eggs

TOPPING
2 oz. flour   1 oz. butter   1 tablespoon caster sugar

Set oven to 350°F or Mark 4. Grease and line a 7 inch flan dish. Roll out the shortcrust pastry on a floured surface and use to line the dish. Mix together the golden syrup, brown sugar, walnuts and eggs. Make the topping by rubbing the butter into the flour and stirring in the caster sugar. Put the syrup mixture on top of the pastry base and then sprinkle evenly with the topping. Bake for approximately 30 minutes.

Chocolate Coconut Fingers

4 oz. margarine or butter   **4 oz. self-raising flour**
2 oz. granulated sugar   **2 oz. desiccated coconut**
2 teaspoons cocoa powder

ICING
4 oz. icing sugar   1 teaspoon cocoa powder   Water to mix

Set oven to 350°F or Mark 4. Grease a 7 inch square shallow tin. Melt the fat and sugar together in a pan. Stir in the flour, coconut and cocoa powder. Press the mixture into the baking tin and bake for 15-20 minutes. Ice immediately with glacé icing made by mixing together the icing sugar, cocoa powder and a little water. Cut into fingers when the icing has set and before the base hardens too much. This simple recipe makes delicious biscuits, ideal for coffee mornings and fêtes.

Salmon Fish Cakes with Cucumber Mayonnaise

FISH CAKES
**8 oz. cold cooked salmon   1 oz. butter   2 oz. onion, finely diced
4 oz. mashed potato   1 egg yolk   1 tablespoon chopped parsley
Salt and pepper**

FOR COATING THE CAKES
**Seasoned flour   1 egg, beaten   Fresh white breadcrumbs
Butter and oil for frying**

CUCUMBER MAYONNAISE
**4 tablespoons mayonnaise   4 tablespoons natural yoghurt
¼ cucumber, peeled and diced**

To make the fish cakes, melt the butter and sauté the onion until transparent. Mix together in a bowl all the fish cake ingredients including the onion. Season well. Shape the mixture into about 8 round, flattened cakes about 1 inch thick. Coat each cake in seasoned flour, beaten egg and finally breadcrumbs. Refrigerate and cook when required by frying in a hot oil and butter mixture. To make the cucumber mayonnaise mix all the ingredients together. Serve the fish cakes hot, together with the mayonnaise and a fresh salad.

Devon Roast Lamb

1 leg of spring lamb, boned out   **Salt and pepper**
2 cloves of garlic, crushed   **1 pint dry cider**
A few sprigs of rosemary   **1-2 tablespoons flour**

Set oven to 425°F or Mark 7. Spread the inside of the leg with garlic, rosemary, salt and pepper and tie with string. Roast for 1 to 2 hours depending on the size of joint and the type of cooked result which is preferred. When cooked, remove the lamb to a serving dish and keep warm. Reserve all the juices in the oven pan, stir in the flour, mix in the cider, return to the stove and boil rapidly until the sauce thickens; season to taste. Garnish the meat with sprigs of rosemary and serve the sauce separately.

Cockington Forge, Torquay

Cheese Crust Vegetable Pie

CHEESE PASTRY
6 oz. flour   ½ teaspoon salt   ½ teaspoon dried mustard powder
4 oz. butter   3 oz. Cheddar cheese, finely grated   Water
VEGETABLE FILLING
3 medium carrots, peeled and diced   6 oz. corn kernels   2 medium onions, finely diced
1 clove garlic, crushed   2 oz. fresh peas   ½ medium swede, peeled and diced
SAUCE
1½ oz. flour   1½ oz. margarine   ¾ pint of milk
Salt and pepper   Dried mixed herbs to taste

Prepare the pastry by the traditional rubbing-in method or in a food processor. Place in the refrigerator to rest. Set oven to 375°F or Mark 5. Place all the vegetables, except the peas, in a large saucepan with 2-3 tablespoons of water, cover and cook gently until tender. Stir in the peas. Make the sauce by melting the margarine, adding the flour and cooking for 2-3 minutes. Remove from the heat and gradually add the milk, beating well between each addition. Return to the heat and, stirring continuously, bring to the boil. Add the vegetables to the sauce with the mixed herbs and season well. Put into a pie dish and immediately cover with the cheese pastry. Bake until the pastry is golden in colour; 35 minutes approximately. The vegetables in this pie can be varied according to what is in season.

Auntie Molly's Strawberry Preserve

2 lb. strawberries   1 lb. redcurrants   2 lb. granulated sugar, warmed

Strawberries are renowned for giving a poor set but, combined with redcurrants which have good setting properties, a delicious and reliable preserve is achieved. Prepare the fruit by hulling and washing the strawberries and removing the redcurrants from their stems and washing. Place the redcurrants in a thick-based pan with very little water and boil rapidly for about 5 minutes until mushy. Add the strawberries and boil gently until soft; approximately 20 minutes. Add the warmed sugar and stir until dissolved. Boil rapidly until setting point is reached. Cool for 15-20 minutes and then pot and cover in warmed jam jars.

Soused Mackerel *from Beer*

6 medium size mackerel   3 bay leaves
1 large onion, peeled and sliced   ¼ pint cider vinegar
16 black peppercorns   ¼ pint water

Set oven to 350°F or Mark 4. Gut and wash the mackerel carefully and place in a large baking dish. Sprinkle over them the onion, peppercorns and bay leaves. Mix together the vinegar and water, pour over the fish and cover the dish with foil. Bake for 25-30 minutes. Allow the fish to cool in the liquid and then lift out with a fish slice. Skin and fillet the fish if desired. Serve with crusty bread and butter, wedges of lemon and a green salad.

Potted Cheese

12 oz. hard cheese, grated
(Cheddar types – there are many produced in Devon – Belstone is a favourite)
4 oz. butter   6 tablespoons dry white wine
4 tablespoons chopped fresh herbs to taste;
chives, thyme and parsley are particularly good

This is an excellent way of using up "bits" left over from the cheese board. Cream the butter in a food processor and add the grated cheese into it. With the processor still going add the wine gradually, a little at a time, and lastly the herbs. Pack the mixture into a round pot. When firm it can be turned out and coated with chopped herbs.

Upcott Pork

2 oz. butter   2 lb. pork tenderloin, sliced thinly
6 oz. Curworthy cheese (or Cheddar), grated
1 small onion, peeled and finely diced
2 medium eating apples, peeled and sliced
½ pint dry cider   ¼ pint double cream   Salt and pepper

Melt the butter in a frying pan and sauté the thin slices of pork for 5 or 6 minutes until cooked through. Place on a hot dish and interleave with layers of grated cheese; set aside and keep warm. Sauté the onions in the same pan, add the apples and cook until soft. Add the cider and, when bubbling, stir in the cream. Cook for 3 or 4 minutes. Season. Pour the sauce over the pork and cheese, and serve.

METRIC CONVERSIONS

The weights, measures and oven temperatures used in the preceding recipes can be easily converted to their metric equivalents. The conversions listed below are only approximate, having been rounded up or down as may be appropriate.

Weights

Avoirdupois	Metric
1 oz.	just under 30 grams
4 oz. (¼ lb.)	app. 115 grams
8 oz. (½ lb.)	app. 230 grams
1 lb.	454 grams

Liquid Measures

Imperial	Metric
1 tablespoon (liquid only)	20 millilitres
1 fl. oz.	app. 30 millilitres
1 gill (¼ pt.)	app. 145 millilitres
½ pt.	app. 285 millilitres
1 pt.	app. 570 millilitres
1 qt.	app. 1.140 litres

Oven Temperatures

	°Fahrenheit	Gas Mark	°Celsius
Slow	300	2	150
	325	3	170
Moderate	350	4	180
	375	5	190
	400	6	200
Hot	425	7	220
	450	8	230
	475	9	240

Flour as specified in these recipes refers to plain flour unless otherwise described.